The Rewards
of a
God Orchestrated Life

The Rewards
of a
God Orchestrated Life

By

Stacy Bannworth and
Millie M. Ricks Kyle

WITH A FOREWORD & INTRODUCTION

By Millie M. Ricks Kyle

XULON PRESS

Xulon Press
2301 Lucien Way #415
Maitland, FL 32751
407.339.4217
www.xulonpress.com

Paperback ISBN-13: 978-1-6628-4223-8
Ebook ISBN-13: 978-1-6628-4261-0

Decatur, Georgia

At 66 years young (now 69), I'm always struck at how God humbles me; as He continues to order my steps and allows me to listen. This beautiful story, that will hold your heart hostage and teach each one of us the rewards of a God orchestrated life. Stacy Bannworth mentioned her story some time ago. However, my focus, at the time, was on completing my college degree.

Unknown to me, she was patient enough to wait on me. God is good. Opportunities, such as this don't come along often. So, it's good to take time to listen, and enjoy the journey only he can guide you through. Often, at the start of a new gifted day, God has placed on my heart that I am joyfully alone.

There is great joy, in assisting this fine God fearing young lady; living a life completely orchestrated by God. If we learn from our mistakes and humble ourselves to the will of God we will be very successful. Stacy is a huge success because she honor's God with her walk in humility and obedience. Success in man's eyes is quite different than in the eyes of God our Lord and Savior. When we truly love our neighbor as we love ourselves, and look beyond circumstance, and see the person, not his skin color, or cultural differences—Then we begin to see one another in a more loving way. And begin to grasp why Jesus died on Calvary, for us all. No one is excluded. Only, when man sees as God would have us to see, will we as a human race really become successful in loving one another.

In closing: All I feel qualified to do is to thank God, for the chance to love Jesus because He first loved me. "For the Bible tells me so…" For God is gracious loving, and merciful it is more than sufficient, for love to saturate the heart, that truly honors and loves the Lord. Stacy is such a person. She loves God with all her heart, mind and soul. This is what gives her the heart and willingness to do all that she can for her fellow man.

Millie M. Ricks Kyle

Introduction

Upon inner reflection, I realize how relevant Stacy Bannworth's story is as the current climate of America and its values are deeply scarred by lack of ability to honor God and Country. Thus, this God fearing young lady's example will serve to help all of us lean not unto our own understanding. In my opinion, she is a shining example of what hope looks like.

- As it is written in the Bible: Trust in the LORD with all thine heart; and lean not unto thine own understanding. In all thy ways acknowledge him, and he shall direct thy paths. —Proverbs 3:5, 6.

- Wait on the LORD: be of good courage, and he shall strengthen thine heart: wait, I say, on the LORD. —Psalm 27:14.

As a mother, writer and a friend Stacy reminds me that her ability to live in a world filled with chaos, a lacking in too many of us to obey the law of the land (certainly not new); her walk of humility and obedience is a needed ingredient in the world.

My level of confidence in what this book will bring to America and our global community is highly elevated. God alone knows which one of us will choose, or reject him. Life is a fragile God given gift to every soul birthed into it. Particularly, when we allow him to take charge; our demeanor becomes more Christ like; forgiving, kind, full of grace, and mercy. Because when we honor his will we allow magical life experiences such as we could not imagine occurring. Thus, we learn to open our hearts to one another's differences embracing them as gifts without fear or jealousy.

However, we can only learn this lesson when we walk in faith honoring God. Stacy appears to know this lesson well. Since, God is in-charge he guides our actions, hearts, mind and soul to the level of love we cannot experience until we know Him. If and when more of us honor and respect each other as he instructs and desires; only then will we really know what real freedom, hope and love is.

In closing: This story is a gift from God to Stacy's life. Therefore, I believe it will be a gift to America and our global community. She is not just an extraordinary woman of God; a wonderful wife, mother, and friend. Stacy's faith is her motivation to help those less fortunate and perhaps to elevate them and the rest of us to step out of our comfort zones, and love each other no matter our circumstances.

Table of Contents

The Rewards of a God Orchestrated Life

1 My World Changed Forever 1

2 Why Does He Want Me to Meet Tammy? . . . 5

3 I Couldn't Get Her Off 7

4 How Can We Help You? 11

5 One Night's Conversation 15

6 Find Them a Home 17

7 I Felt Ashamed 21

8 Little Did We Know...? 25

9 Again, a God Thing 29

1

My World Changed Forever

O n January 26, 2013, my world changed forever. Let me explain, through God's direction, a major blessing was presented into my life. I attend a wonderful Baptist Church in McDonough, Georgia and I'm a member of a life group called Restored and Redeemed.

Our life group consists of 40 couples that have been remarried due to death of a spouse, divorce, or couples affected by divorce in their families. All I can say, is they are a wonderful group of people that honestly, I call my friends.

All of us felt led by God.

During one of our class meetings, I was asked to organize activities for group participation. All of us felt led by God to do some form of outreach in our community.

We had been advised of some homeless people living in nearby Henry County. Most of the people were being housed in extended stay motels. Therefore, we decided to collect funds as a class and chose a Saturday to go out and feed God's people.

As the organizer and planner, I was responsible for handling the money; purchasing the food, organizing the place we would prepare the food, and where we would meet to distribute the food. I say this because my only expectation was to feed God's people on that day.

However, little did I know, what additional plans God had on his agenda for me on that fateful day. On January 25, 2013, a small group of us met at one of those Clubs you can buy in bulk; in order to make all the purchases we would need to feed over 100 people.

Collectively, we decided the menu would consist of: Chili, sandwiches, chips, a cookie and some tea.

It is January 2013.

Upon arriving home that night, I prepared the chili. The next day we met at a group member's home in order to prepare the rest of the items on the menu.

After the food was prepared, we gathered in the yard for prayer lead by our life group leader. His exact words, "Go not expecting anything in return, just love on people." After that we drove over to Stockbridge and parked behind a nearby restaurant.

We fed about 10 people there; some were homeless, and living in the woods. Then we moved up to a nearby, extended stay motel and fed more. We were guided across the street to a motel, under the direction of a kind and gentle man named Bill.

He has been working in this ministry for years. And knew many of the people staying in these extended stay motels. And advised me, that normally the motel management would never give out room numbers. However, they would tell him, how many people might be in need of a meal. Thus, allowing us to leave the meals at the front desk, for those in need.

2

Why Does He Want Me
to Meet Tammy?

With nearly 40 people out in the parking lot; setting up the tables, in preparation of meal delivery. Bill and I walked into the hotel lobby, where he asked the lady working behind the desk; how many meals were needed? She said, "a lot of people had moved out." But, did give us about five room numbers.

As we were turning to leave, Bill turned back around and said, "Oh is Tammy still here?" The lady said, "Oh, yeah, I forgot about her, she's in room 516." Little did I know, what affect those four words "I forgot about her..." would mean to my life. Bill gave me a glance of intensity as if oh, yeah. As he said, "I want Stacy to meet Tammy." And he kept repeating it over and over again. I remember thinking, out of the 40 people in this parking lot— Why does he want me to meet Tammy?

3

I Couldn't Get Her Off...

I would quickly find out what God's plan was. As we walked to the room, he told me, Tammy is a 42-year-old female with stage 3 breast cancer; with two children living in the motel with her. He said, if we could, he'd like us to give them some extra meals.

This Fragile Timid Young Lady Appears.

So, we arrived at Tammy's door and knocked and to our surprise, this fragile timid young lady appears. Wearing a hooded jacket, that covers her head; so, we can't see her hair is gone. Bill introduced me and five others in our team to Tammy. We talked and prayed with her.

She was so humbled and overwhelmed by our act of kindness; causing her to sob as she thanked us for coming. While we were talking, her 26-year-old son drove-up with his 11-year-old sister. We greeted them, and gave them the extra food to take inside.

We said our goodbyes, promised to pray for Tammy and her family. The usual, "I'll be praying for you." I would come to realize, there was more to that statement.

Our life group had plans that night to go out to dinner and fellowship. However, I couldn't get Tammy off my mind during the entire meal. At one point, during the meal, my dad called me, to ask a question.

Since, Tammy was so heavy on my heart; I shared a little with him about her prior to hanging-up.

Upon arriving home, later that evening, my dad called again. He wanted to know more about Tammy, it was weighing heavy on his heart as well. I told him what I knew, which wasn't much.

My dad said, "We need to help this lady." My response, 'I'm feeling the same way.' I told him, that I would go back to the extended stay motel the next day. Perhaps, I could talk with her and find out what her needs are.

4

How Can We Help You?

So, that Sunday my husband and I drove back to the motel and knocked on her door. Tammy opened the door and I reminded her of our meeting the day before. She said, she remembered us being there. I asked her 'How can we help you?' She said, "I just want a Home." And expressed that she was tired of living in a motel with her children.

Well, needless to say, I didn't know how to pull that off. However, as we talked, she informed me of a mobile home park; that she had actually visited with a lady named Barbara. The problem was she didn't have the money it would take to get her in it. She had no income and her son was only working a part-time job. They were paying $228.00 per week to stay in the motel.

With the current weeks rent due on Thursday, no money to pay it, and the threat of being kicked out. I was feeling; how can she heal, much less rest peaceably at night, with such dread looming in her head.

We asked her about immediate needs, such as food and clothing to ease her mind a bit. She gave us sizes of clothing the children needed, she was not concerned about herself. In her opinion, she had let her children down by not being able to provide a decent home for them. Never faced with anything quite like this my feelings of empathy were heightened.

Tammy told us, how she had gotten sick and felt the doctor misdiagnosed her condition as menopause and depression. Therefore, prescribed her a drug called Prempro that had a class action lawsuit, for causing breast cancer. Because of her illness Stage-three breast Cancer, she was forced to go on FMLA from her job.

Upon her return to her work, she was advised by her employer, that she was actually due back three days prior. Thus, she was terminated, for failure to return to work. Due to her job loss and having no income; she lost her home and all its contents. With no clear choice at hand, she was forced to move into an extended living situation and remained there for about seven months.

Don't Know the Exact Moment We Knew We Were Friends...

Since, I had never faced anything quite like this my feelings of empathy were heightened. Tammy is basically out of options, no quick fixes; now forced to seek the support of Atlanta's Legal Aid team, in order to get the much-needed disability compensation.

Even though, Tammy and I only just met, a bond was felt as we kept going to the motel several nights a week; bringing food, clothing and paying the motel bill twice. I don't know the exact moment we knew we were friends, but that's what happened.

5

One Nights'
Conversation Stood Out

As Tammy and I shared stories of our childhoods, marriages, family and children. One night's conversation stood out vividly in my mind. My husband and I returned to the motel; after a lovely dinner. During this particular encounter, with Tammy: While my husband entertained Heather with a game they were playing on his phone.

Tammy and I were talking: She shared the very painful loss of her mother to cervical cancer in 2001. I learned her mother was her best friend. At the time, Tammy was expecting Heather; understandably, she took the loss extremely hard. Of course, as anyone can imagine, this life altering event caused a great deal of stress on her pregnancy.

When Heather was born, the doctor told Tammy that she was her miracle baby and should not have lived. So, Tammy decided to give her miracle baby the middle name of Angel; because, she felt that Heather was her angel, sent down from heaven to help her through the deep loss of her mother.

After hearing that story, I was choked-up and started crying; you see I have a cousin named Angel, who at birth weighed less than one pound and the doctors told her parents that she was a miracle baby.

Unfortunately, she only lived to be 16-years-old, when she was killed in a car accident, driven by a drunk driver. This happened six months prior to our meeting. Certainly, hearing her story, made it clear to me our meeting was not by chance. It's amazing to me that God in his infinite wisdom allowed our paths to cross knowing our history; two miracle babies, both with the middle names of Angel.

I Need You to Be My Hands and My Feet.

Of course, he already knew about the two Angels; and that one-day Tammy and I would meet and share these stories. After this, I knew that God was saying help this family; I need you to be my hands and my feet.

6

Find Them a Home

Then, the next day at work, I found myself thinking 'What can I do; What would Jesus want me to do?' I kept feeling him say, find them a Home. Wow! God, how do I pull this off? I knew, he would show me the way and he did.

I started calling around to mobile home parks in the Henry County area. Asking what was available and how much a mobile home would cost. My dad and I were scheduled to go and look at a mobile home, in a mobile home community in McDonough, GA in a few days. When I received a call from a nearby mobile home park, in Stockbridge, GA in Henry County. They advised me that they had a mobile home that they would give me free of charge.

Since, the current owner just wanted to get it off his hands, and get out of the Lot Rent. I said, 'Free, you are giving me a free mobile home for Tammy?' To which the lady replied, "yes, it does need some work though," as she advised me to come by and pick-up the keys and have a look at it. Also, to let her know if I wanted it and all that Tammy would have to pay is the Lot Rent.

God had a plan that was bigger than my discouragement.

So, I went by and picked-up the keys with my dad as support to look at it. It was in terrible shape, the floors were torn-up, walls colored, just unsightly all around. My dad and I looked at each other with a sigh of despair and said, "Is this fixable and how much would the repairs cost?"

We were somewhat discouraged by what we'd seen. But, God had a plan that was bigger than my discouragement. While attending church service, the following Sunday; during our class, I stood up in front and told everyone about Tammy. And what God was leading me to do.

At the end of the class, a life group classmate introduced himself. He had been attending the class for the past three weeks. And advised me, that he owned a construction business and would be glad to come and take a look at the mobile home. I said, that would be great and we met that very afternoon at the mobile home.

When we walked in; he saw what I could not. He had a vision of what it could be, as he said, "this is doable; I can fix this up in two to 3 weeks, at no charge." I said, 'What no charge?!'

Needless to say, I was at a loss for words. He explained, to me that he knew people that would donate their labor, materials and time, for his family. God planted this seed and we were to make it happen. He said, "All I need you to do is furnish the place." I said, 'I can do that.'

Immediately, I made phone calls to people requesting donations of furniture and household goods, receiving so much that I had to turn some away! There were enough beds, for Tammy and both of the children, and living room furniture almost brand new.

We truly witnessed a blessing.

On February 20, 2013, my husband and four others worked all day putting the place together. The end result, the place was gorgeous—we were thrilled.

Welcome home balloons were placed outside. Then, Tammy along with some life group classmates and two friends were brought to her new home at 9:00 pm.

7

I Felt Ashamed...

I will never forget the look on Tammy's face when she saw the mobile home for the first time. She said, "This is a mansion, this is the nicest place I have ever lived."

As she embraced me she started to cry. Later, she said to me, she felt as if I were her angel. And that she prayed to God on January 25, 2013, to send someone to help her and her family. Because she was tired of living in the motel and having feelings of hopelessness.

It was on January 26, 2013, He sent me to her door. Just goes to show, that God hears our prayers. He certainly heard Tammy's. She loved her new home that God provided for her. It was a very emotional night for all of us involved. I went home feeling so blessed by all that God orchestrated in using me.

We truly witnessed a blessing.

However, while pausing in the mirror, I felt ashamed; because, I never thought of my home as a mansion, and I have a lovely home. I have never been in a homeless situation; therefore, I was truly broken and humbled by all that God had revealed through this experience. He allows growth in every human encounter.

On February 21, 2013, Tammy and her family moved into their new home. Tammy was so very happy. There was a commitment from friends, including a couple of my life group classmates to pay the electric bill for one year.

My Life Group classmates agreed to pay the Lot Rent for a couple of months. And my husband and I would cover the cable, gas and phone bill until Tammy's disability money was received and or Robby located a full-time job.

Tammy and Robby signed their lease with the mobile home park and everything was good to go. My husband took Robby to look for a job two days later, so he could help contribute to the house-hold expenses. They stopped in a nearby Staples store, where Robby decided to complete an employment application.

While he was filling it out the manager; approached him, and asked him what type of work was he looking for? Robby said, "anything you might have open." To which the manager responded, by asking him to return the next day, for an interview at 3:00 pm.

Robby returned the next day, for the interview and was hired an hour afterwards and started the very next day. Again, a God thing. In our economy, it is hard to find a job within months, much less 24 hours of going out to look for one.

Things appeared to be going great. Soon Tammy received money due her and was advised her disability money would start on April 1, 2013.

Since God knows all things; during one of Tammy's chemo treatments she learned the cancer had spread to her bones. Thus, even though, she appeared to be feeling better and more mobile around her home. There was no real improvement.

During one of my visits, we discussed what would be her wishes for Heather; who would be responsible for her? Now, the reality of her predicament is clear to us all. Her response was, "I don't know, I don't have anyone." So, my husband and I offered, to be Heather's guardians and raise her for Tammy.

In mid-March my husband and I went down to the office of Atlanta Legal Aid and met with a kind representative regarding the need to set-up a will and guardianship papers. Tammy told the representative her wishes and the papers were drawn-up.

8

Little Did We Know How Soon?

On Easter Sunday, which fell on the 31st of March in 2013, Tammy asked if she and Heather could attend church service with us. Of course, I said yes and told her what time we would pick them up for the service. Tammy looked so beautiful, lovely make-up, exquisite dress and her hair fixed beautifully—she was glowing. Once in the church, we ended up sitting in the front row, near the baptism pool.

Also, near a few of our friends, who had remodeled her home; Tammy was excited to be near the baptism pool. Listening intently, to the pastor's message that morning. The message was entitled: "This is Our Temporary Home and our permanent home is with Jesus." Tammy cried the entire time, causing me to reach over and embrace her as she said, "I know, I'm a big baby." I said, 'No, you're being led by the Holy Spirit.'

Afterwards, the pastor gave the plan of salvation. Asking all those in attendance if they have given their lives over to the Lord, to raise their hand; Tammy's flew-up. After the service, Tammy met briefly with the pastor. She advised him of her situation, and that she wanted to be baptized. Afterwards, she met with an elder to find out how to prepare, for her baptism the following Sunday.

Tammy was so excited, to make her declaration of faith. After such an emotional and lovely service; all of us went home, and had a wonderful Easter dinner together. Tammy's contribution was a bunny cake and cookies. While we were all together, God kept pressing on my heart, to talk with Heather and ask her if she would like to come to Florida with us, for Spring Break the next day.

At first, I hesitated about it, then, I gave into the feeling I was having. As my husband took Tammy and Heather home, to pick up clothes for the trip. Tammy rested for a short time; afterwards, she did some shopping with a friend returning home around 10:00 p.m. Upon her return, she laid down to rest.

The next morning, we packed the car and headed for Florida. My mom came in and said, "I thought you weren't taking Heather?" I said, 'Mommy, someday she might be mine.' Little did I know how soon; there again, a God thing. We were about two hours out, when my mom received a call from my aunt, saying that Tammy had passed away in her sleep. Robby found her in her bed.

My mom, told my husband to pull the car over and we got out as she told us. It took all the God given strength in me, to keep from crying in front of Heather (she's in the car). We decided to wait until we arrive back home, before breaking the news to Heather.

So, we turned around and went back home so that we could make the arrangements. It was the longest ride back. We told the kids we had a family emergency to tend to. Once arriving back to my dad's home; because it was across from Tammy's.

Once, inside, I sat Heather on my lap and said, 'Do you remember how Pastor Tim, said that this is our temporary home and our permanent home is with Jesus Christ.' She said, "yes." I said, 'well, that's where your mommy is now. She passed away in her sleep last night.' Immediately, she started screaming and crying. As I held her close and told her it was going to be okay.

9

Again, a God Thing

I asked my husband to go and get Robby from next
door and he came over and they embraced each
other. Moments later, Tammy's brother showed up
with his girlfriend. All of us sat down and discussed
Tammy's wishes and making the arrangements.
Tammy wanted to be cremated. Once at the funeral
home, I requested that her remains be taken and
arrangements were made for the cremation.

Once there, we were permitted a viewing for about
twenty minutes. As my husband and I discussed,
what we should do. We knew Tammy would not
have wanted us to cancel our Spring break plans.
So, we went to Florida, to get our minds off things.

Finally, I saw why God wanted me to take Heather
with us to Florida, because she would have been

in the bed lying next to her deceased mother. As I spent time on the beach, reflecting on a gracious Father and thinking how he orchestrated all of this. His plan, not mine, down to every amazing detail.

I felt so blessed to be a part of his plan for Tammy's life and mine. Then, I think of what the alternative could have been for Tammy. The possibility of passing away in a motel, or in a car. Just the thought of it is heartbreaking.

It warms my heart, knowing that God used me to provide her a home. Where she was able to lay her head down, close her eyes one last time before she made her final journey to join Him. Heather was able to enjoy her time at the beach.

Returning home, we moved all of Heather's belongings over to our home in her new room. Then, we cleaned out all of the things in Tammy's room. Robby decided to stay in the mobile home.

He was now responsible for the lot rent and utilities; at least until he located a really responsible roommate; who pays the lot rent, while Robby pays the utilities, a perfect arrangement: Again, a God thing.

Now, it was time to prepare a small memorial service for Tammy to remember her life—I knew she would appreciate that. So, I contacted an Elder at the church, to help with the arrangements of a fitting memorial service, for her in the music suite; he officiated at the service. Several attendees spoke about Tammy and we showed a video.

My Life Group classmates provided the food for the friends and family members that attended. It was a lovely celebration of Tammy's life. I know she would have loved it.

Guardianship & New School

Soon, we applied for guardianship, and placed Heather into a new school. As I'm thinking; now where will that be? Tammy's words came to mind, "Wouldn't it be wonderful if Heather could go to the same wonderful school with Lauren?" That was her prayer. Well, little did I know, that the church would answer Tammy's prayer?

I called the school and inquired about scholarships and was told that they do not have scholarships; however, they do have financial aid. This was a huge blessing. A kind admissions representative said, she would check on that and get back to me.

Divinely guided, I'm sure, she called back the very next day; informing me that after talking with the pastor, a full scholarship was offered to Heather. With all tuition paid, we only had to pay the matriculation and lunch fees. Wow! Again a God thing.

We were advised of uniform resale day, meaning uniforms were used but in good condition. Mentioning this situation to my boss while preparing to leave early, to make a purchase for Heather. My boss handed me $100.00, stating, "I hope this helps in getting uniforms for Heather."

Now with orientation day upon us, we took Heather to meet her teachers and find her classes. The last class was held in the music suite. As we walk in, I started remembering the beautiful memorial service for Tammy and so did Heather.

She says, "Isn't this where we had my Mom's memorial service." I said, 'yes I know.' Then we met her teacher and I filled her in on the situation and told her 'I don't think Heather is going to be able to come into this classroom every day.' To which she responded, "I'll take care of it." As Heather began to cry, the teacher embraced her and advised her that she would try to get the classroom changed; and she made it happen before the first day of classes. Again, a God thing.

A wonderful school with loving compassionate people. Heather started school and it has been a roller-coaster ride for all of us. We've prayed a lot regarding Heather moving into our home, and incorporating her into our lives including her adjustment to her new life.

Of course, with lots of counseling and prayer, God is working out the bumps in this highway of life. What a true blessing He bestowed upon my family.

For Example:

Some days, I say 'Really, God, Me. Who am I? Who am I, to be the hands and the feet of such a wonderful Lord who walked this earth leading a sinless life?' When you ask, he shows you. He will definitely, get your attention.

For example: Three years before this adventure, my husband and I decided we wanted to adopt a foster child. So, we went through DFACS, went through all the training required. Searched for a little girl, we prayed often for her. Between the ages of eleven or 12 years old.

After two years of looking, we decided to give-up and let God take the helm. Maybe that wasn't God's plan for our life, at that time. Now, we know it was because he already knew that Heather would be with us, and when. So, sometimes you have to stop and be still. Be still and let God handle things.

That is one lesson I've learned from this. Life is going to get messy and that's okay. As long as you seek God first, for the small, and the big stuff in your life; you will be alright. Wow, how life takes us through a journey. Don't expect easy.

Today, we are still making it work. Supporting each other, loving each other as we continue to grow as a family; learning about each other. Robby and Heather may not be my biological children, but they are my brother and sister in Christ. And Christ calls us to help and love each other with all our heart.

Finally, I love my family deeply. I hope and pray this story inspires you to step out on faith and let God orchestrate your life.

When he calls you to do something, listen and don't be afraid. Don't say, "God, I can't, it's out of my comfort zone." Trust me, I know. I was out of my comfort zone — but, not Gods' I was right in line

with his comfort zone and His mission for my life—
just wait, God has a mission for you too...

———————